THE SAME MAN

PITT POETRY SERIES

Nancy Krygowski and Jeffrey McDaniel, *Editors*

THE SAME MAN BOBBY ELLIOTT

Winner
of the
*Agnes Lynch
Starrett Poetry
Prize*

Published by the University of Pittsburgh Press, Pittsburgh, Pa., 15260

Copyright © 2025, Bobby Elliott

Manufactured in the United States of America

Printed on acid-free paper

10 9 8 7 6 5 4 3 2 1

ISBN 13: 978-0-8229-6749-1

ISBN 10: 0-8229-6749-9

Cover photo by Steve Shreve via Unsplash

Cover design and book design by Alex Wolfe

Publisher: University of Pittsburgh Press, 7500 Thomas Blvd., 4th floor, Pittsburgh, PA 15260, United States, www.upittpress.org

EU Authorized Representative: Easy Access System Europe, Mustamäe tee 50, 10621 Tallinn, Estonia, gpsr.requests@easproject.com

for Victoria, Jamie, and Peter

CONTENTS

THE SAME MAN

MONDEGREEN

I mistake the sound of a recycling cart
hitting the curb

for the latch of our gate
and picture him instantly:

my father stumbling
into the light of the backyard

to shoot himself.

I'd been looking at the fruit trees
and the fire pit,

the loose board of the old fence
in the wind.

I'd been thinking of how lost
you'd have to be

to believe you knew
everything there was to know

about yourself.
And now this sound

I mistake for my father
going through with it: one

awful letter in his coat pocket
to me, another

to my unborn son.

THE FALL OF 1990

Depending on whose word
you trust, the rain
was either tapering off

or coming down so hard
it sounded like fruit
on the roof of our car.

In one version
it took us an hour
to find a parking spot.

In the other
we circled the block
once and there

it was—waiting
right out front.
We loved Boston,

we were just ready
for a change.
Or: *We had a month*

to settle up
and leave.
We left

any way you tell it—
omens everywhere
or signs of mercy,

even light,
as we pulled up,
got out, stood

like a family
in the city's palm.
We were a family—

my father held
my sister's hand
and I bobbed

like a buoy
in my mother's arms.

BILLS

I remember when the lights
used to go out. The sun
untangling itself

like a shoelace
above the trees
and my father

running late.
I remember the money
vanishing but not

where I'd kept it—
the black heels
of the eviction lady,

my mother's maiden name
in her mouth.

SCHOOL NIGHTS

From one couch
to another, she used to tell him

Pick on someone else tonight
because I'm not going to be

your punching bag—
the living room

erupting in laughter,
of all things,

then muted
by tears she was tired

of having to shed
while Vanna White glittered

in the night's sequined gown
and a bank of consonants

and vowels waited
to be touched.

INITIATION

I'd just learned to swim
when he taught me
to float face down
in the pool. The idea
was to hold my breath
and relax, limb to limb,
until someone, ideally
my mother, looked
up from their weight
loss magazine
in horror. Four or five,
I studied him
first, grinned
until his body
looked like a leaf
minding its own
finished business.
At the time, I didn't
know he wanted
to die. The allure
of the ocean not
what it spit back out
but what it kept.

He was so proud
when I did
as I was told,
coming up
for air only after
my mother felt
like she'd slipped
down a flight
of stairs, and he stood
in the oversized
t-shirt he wore
to hide his stomach,
beaming like we
finally had something
in common.

GAME PLAN

He was always after reassurance
that he was a good father

and that no—*of course not*—
we didn't want anyone else

to take his place.
There was never time

to hesitate, to waver, his life,
it seemed, always in the balance

and his children, us,
always the ones to save him,

to talk him down, to game plan
when he wasn't in the room.

Nothing's changed—
when he writes to ask

if we're angry with him
and if we think he's been a failure

he doesn't want
the truth. He wants us to know

there's a gun
he's been holding to his head

and the only reason he's alive
is the two of us.

We are meant to feel loved
by this, not accused.

MAN AT THE BAR

What he wants us to know
is this: the drive home
takes two hours on a good night.
Sometimes he sleeps
on the side of the road,
sometimes he finds himself
standing in his son's room
at four in the morning—
stars on the sky's breath,
a nice whiskey on his.

If it's true, that two people
can make it work,
he's not the right person
to ask. He thinks now
they were never happy
and looks at us—inseparable
as we'll ever be, hanging
on every word—
like my father might have
if we were strangers

in the '90s: briefly,
before going quiet—
the bar filling up quick,
the music starting
any minute now.

SOUNDS

The wind in the trees and on the water.
The radiator waking up in the morning
and after work. The onions on the stove
and the tea kettle getting ready
to go off. Donny Hathaway making it seem
like it's not all that heavy, even if it is,
and ten pairs of sneakers like birds
on the televised court. There are sounds I love
and some I could let go of if I had to,
but it's the one of you walking naked
on the hardwood floors, between the rooms
behind me, that makes me jealous
of the floor itself, of the mirrors you pass
and the clothes in a warm pile on the bed,
the hot water from the shower falling
from your body like a completed thing,
like an apple or an orange, back down
the well of the earth.

WHEN I AM NOT THINKING
OF MY FATHER

And whether
he has a gun
to his head,

I am thinking
of driving you home
from the hospital—

stopping at a yellow,
refusing to turn
on a red,

our three-month old
Baby on Board!
sticker finally

come true:
our newborn
beside you

in the back seat,
manger of light
in the mirror.

PRODROMAL

After sending us home
twice, your pain

somehow not
intolerable enough,

they take us in.
It's a Sunday, the hospital

quiet as a failing
business—the nurses yawning

at their stations,
the doctors off somewhere

dreaming of being paged.
In our minds, he'll be born

by nightfall, a Virgo,
which means nothing

except that he'll be loyal,
analytical and kind

with, I am told, a penchant
for worry and a real feel

for being critical.
In truth, there's a word

for this kind of labor
and though no one

uses it, it explains the next
hours without

progress, the pain
a 9, then a 10 that holds

all night. All night
you wade

into the body's
flooded house

to reach him.

GOING HOME

Mary tells us to cherish every inch
of you, from the bruise
the vacuum left to the toes
I count twice, and maybe it's fear

that has us weeping
in the doorway, maybe
it's joy—your life
in our hands now

no one else's as we smile
for the photograph, our first
as a family, then hurry
to the car, a virus

on the loose and the sky
so thick with wildfire smoke
it's a miracle we make it
home, our neighbors

watching from their
windows as we whisk
you in, brushing ash
like snow from your blanket.

NEW PARENTS

As soon as you're born, we picture ourselves
dying, stepping between you

and whatever could possibly barrel
toward us in the rain—a stolen

pickup truck, a wave pausing
at its crest and asking

for a volunteer. The instinct
in the water now, the blood. Not

that the world cares
or that you—oblivious

in your swaddle we've managed
to put on backward—need

anything but milk. We fantasize
about ending up

on the news—*New
Parents Drown, Save*

Infant Boy—to avoid
imagining this house

ever without you. *Jamie*
we mutter in the mirror, *Jamie*

we call out in our sleep.

LULLABY

Though I'm not supposed to
I look into your eyes at bedtime, still crossed
and figuring out their color, bordering

on closing—then opening again
to our delight and dismay, sleepless
and in love as we are, swaying

like only new parents can:
endlessly, a little mechanically.
The dimmed light and white noise

doing a number not on you
but us. Our eyes heavy
as the rain, and yours, why

I started writing this poem in the first place,
yours now blue but bound
for whatever hills they're bound for,

now crossed but slowly getting it
together, moving in unison
on occasion, I look into them

to make up for all the moons
I've missed, all the bald eagles
I should've stopped for, *ooing*

and *aahing* like everyone else
on their Sunday morning walk
around the reservoir, singing

the song we will never stop
singing, even when you're
deep into your adolescence

and plotting your escape,
even when you're slamming
your bedroom door or crashing

our only car or calling us
motherfuckers, you beautiful,
beautiful boy.

SKIN TO SKIN

After nursing
you're handed off

to me—*Dad*, *Daddy*,
Papa, the name we've yet

to settle on—
and this morning

my skin on yours
puts you right to sleep.

Or, my skin's
a decent enough replica

to keep you sleeping,
milk balming

your lips.
In the first dream

I have about you
I leave the station

alone, checking my pockets
as if you're a wallet

or phone. Your wail
in the distance,

my heart's four
alarm system

going off.
How can I blame you

then or now
for clinging

to your mother's
warmth, her unceasing

light? This morning
after nursing

she hands you off,
sleeping, to me,

your skin on mine
inconceivable

to the city kid
I once was: my parents

having it out
in their bedroom,

my sister's soon
to be jailed

boyfriend climbing
the fire escape

to hers.

TOGETHER

You asked me if I could think back
to a time when they seemed happy

and I can't. As a kid, I'd listen to them
fight like it was an album I couldn't

get out of my head: standing, at first,
in the shallows of the sound,

then wading out further, deeper.
The city went on as it always did:

someone rolled down their window
to tell someone else to go

fuck themselves, a boy's mother
dragged him by his sleeve

across the street. I would put my ear
to their door like a stethoscope.

I would hold my breath for as long
as I could without drowning.

INVENTORY CONTROL

When they finally let him go
he wasn't supposed to be ecstatic

but he was. He hated his job so much
he sounded like Levine

at Ford Rouge—the grind
unbearable, an insult

he had to stomach for 25 years
while his siblings bought

beach houses and second cars, pitied
and hated my father at the same time.

He was going to be a painter,
at least that's what he told me

growing up: he'd gone to art school
but dropped out after a semester,

threw away every canvas he'd ever
touched. Except for the one hanging

above the counter in his childhood
home. I don't remember

what it was, only that I stood
in front of it every time I visited

after the divorce. A watercolor
probably, a landscape,

the only thing I want when he's gone.

BIG WAVE SURFER

He mentions his three children
in passing, so we never learn
their names or how old they were
when he quit his job
and started surfing. The story,
the documentary's sure, is about
the ocean, but I keep wondering
if it isn't about a man
leaving his family. The allure
of the waves in Nazaré
not only their scale but how far
they take him from home,
how easy they make it
to have an affair. All we see
is swell after giant swell,
the footage almost
mesmerizing enough
to admire him—left
by his own father, beaten
by a stepfather, now
the world's greatest living
big wave surfer cheered on
by a woman half his age, the film

in love with how they keep
his dream of scaling 9
and 10 story tall waves alive,
how they start their own
beautiful family. And how ready
he finally is to change
a diaper, to make it look
effortless and humble,
like muscle memory.

WE HOLD EACH OTHER IN THE KITCHEN

We hold each other in the kitchen
so he can see us

from the highchair,
his parents rested

in a past life and swaying
to the music he likes

to overhear
while eating each

meticulous seed
of the pomegranate

and pointing
to the picture of his

grandfather smiling
on the fridge.

I was a toddler
when the bills started

piling up on the dresser
and the owner

of the market my mother
bought diapers

and cold cuts from
with bounced checks

approached my father
quietly in the parking lot—

and only after months
of watching us

walk out
like we were good

for it. I don't know where
my face is

in my son's.
I don't know how my parents

ever stood in the produce
aisle again. I don't know

if the stars
populate the sky

like tumors
on a scan. I know

the sound they made
when they fought.

I know how afraid
we are to raise

our voices. I know
a sweetness

in us was once
in them.

WEEKEND GETAWAY

Not *ocean* or *bird* or *Daddy*
but *Papaw* he keeps

repeating on the beach,
my grandfather's name

now my father's—
my son hoping

he's just stuck
in traffic. *Ocean*

I say and point
to the tide making

and remaking
its bed—*ocean*

—but he wants
his grandfather to say it

with us, to witness
his first wet

fistful of sand.
Do I wince

because I'm jealous
or am I forgiven

for going quiet?
I stand between him

and the wind jutting
north, his red raincoat

flapping
like a weatherman's,

his loyalty
to each syllable

a coincidence—I
tell myself

as if I'm unaware
of my own love

for the same man.

HARMLESS

1.

He used to tell us
to visit the Daddy Store

and pick out someone else
if we were so unhappy.

It was one of his go-to moves
like telling my mother

she was just like her mother
so might as well live

thousands of miles away, too.
He liked to suggest candidates—

Arcadio Casillas, Bill Strong—
fathers who were known

to throw whiskey glasses
and haymakers

at their children, our friends,
making him look

if not saintly, harmless
in comparison.

2.

I always imagined
the store aisled

like any other
with a clearance section

in the back, full
of fathers set

to expire by the weekend
and, there

for a reason, hiding
from the kids like us

standing side by side
in the makeshift light.

3.

But say we did,
say, after listening

to him dare us
to choose,

we decided
what was best

for the family
was a new father,

there was no
Daddy Store

to return him to.
There was only

the consequence
of coming clean

and being left
with no father

at all—ours
going on and on

about how naive
we were to think

we had it bad
and how soon

we'd learn
the grass wasn't

ever greener,
that our friends

were beat
with serving spoons

and the thick
end of pool cues

and yet
we were the ones

complaining.
What we wanted

was someone
who let us be

a family. What
he wanted, fished

for relentlessly,
was an excuse

to pack his shit
and go.

REDMOND TELLS ME
WHAT I FEEL

is not to be confused
with anger. That when I
look back at the great
bouts of my childhood
or my father hugs me
just to get it over with
or I hear him in
the living room pleading
with my one-year-old
and I imagine the day
I'm asked to help him
dress and take pills,
all the nouns fleeing
like all the men
he always used to watch
being chased on TV,
the audio picking up the
swishing sound of a
maniacal cop's blue
uniform, the word
I'm looking for
is rage.

WHAT WE SEE TOGETHER

Always the trees, always the crows
on the power lines dripping
like an old shower head. Cats
on occasion—one-eared,
tagless—roses
and toddlers breaking out
into a sprint. The minister
and his wife arriving
hand in hand, the church
perennially in need
of a new coat. Yards abandoned
and yards resplendent—
both of us drawn like a bath
to the statue of St. Francis.
Palms of rain, palms of ash,
palms the squirrels
leap to and leave trembling
like a glass. The light
at the base of the maple. The painter
in her studio unknown
and painting. The plane
making you crane your neck
in the stroller. The sunflower,

the mailman. The house
with its fading picture
of a missing child
in the window. The final block home:
our overgrown plum trees
always with more fruit,
our front door and the woman
who brought you into this world
hour by seasick hour
on the other side of it, always
waiting, always what makes you
smile before the door even opens.

PHOTOGRAPHS

My sister thinks
they're a way
for him
to live in the past

but I think
it's an attempt
to rewrite it:
every inch

of wall space
taken up
by my smile
and hers,

by Jamie's
and Maya's
and Violet's.
Even his siblings

make an appearance
in the hall
as if
their falling out

was fiction.
We don't
come over often.
When we do

I'm struck
by how sad
it is
to see myself

as a boy—
my left
front tooth
browning

in the light,
every dollar
I'd saved
lifted

from the shoebox
I didn't think
to hide—
as my own

son shakes
the city
I grew up in
until snow

swirls
around it
and I picture
my father

listening
at my door
to make sure
I was asleep.

THE SAME MAN

He's been good all year
when our entrées come out
like a reward

for reinvention
and he finally says
what he's always said—

that his life wouldn't
be worth living
without us

which is another way
of saying
he'd kill himself

if not for the few
hours each week he gets
to play hide

and seek with my
son, who always
picks the same spot

behind the couch,
laughing as my father
walks right past him

nailing the part
of the duped
like he was born

to disappoint everyone
but his grandchildren,
born to spoil them

and hold them,
to caw like a crow
one minute and rumble

like a vintage yellow
motorcycle the next,
$45,000 in debt

and a new gun
in the safe.
The same man

who mastered the art
of making
my mother cry

and left me
a set of his keys
so I'd be the one

to find him
in the bathroom
of his second floor walk-up

on Main, to search
for a pulse and put
both hands

to his chest,
trying to remember
how deep to go,

how soon to breathe,
how often I tried
to convince him

to stay. Even the night
of my wedding,
even now

I pitch therapy
and a summit
with each sibling

he's told off,
order a dessert
I'm too embarrassed

to maul the name
of, pointing to it
with a smile

our waiter almost
forgives and agreeing
when my father leans

into the candlelight
to say *We can*
tell each other anything,

can't we? My mind
going to that year
in college I stood

outside the dorm
my new friends
were partying in,

trying to decipher
what I was hearing
over the phone—

the wind chimes
on the back deck
going wild, his two

untrained dogs
barking, the chamber
opening, the chamber

closing, something
about why I had to be
so far away.

BEFORE ANYONE ELSE KNEW

We spent a weekend on the coast
and walked as far as we could

into what I imagine was fog
or mist that wouldn't let up

until the spring. You were our
fragile son or daughter (daughter

if you asked me then), future
we toasted sparkling

apple cider to in the evening, TV-less
and cooking Bolognese in a dented

stock pot someone went
to town on once, like the flute

I ruined in the 7th grade, year
of smoke touching down

on the moon of my lungs, year
the towers fell and we sang

by candlelight at the precinct. What
I'm saying is we coveted

that brief period of time
when you were a secret

and only ours to envision
on the drive and on the beach,

in our arms and in the night.
How different it is now

—sweet boy standing
in the dark of your room

and trying to remember to call
for us before crying—

to keep the same secret
from you, a brother.

PRAYED FOR

When he asks about names
for our second, I know better

than to share but share
anyway—I give him

Saul, the latest addition
to the longlist, a name I heard

on the radio, driving to work,
surprised we hadn't

thought of it already,
a name that makes my father

wince like he's just
watched my first born

press his wet finger
into an outlet.

But that's a Jewish name
he says with that look

he used to shoot
my mother when he wanted her

to stop breathing.
How about Adam?

The joke lost
on him as Jamie

calls for me
from the yard,

rain boots dotted
with dinosaurs

and dew, and a worm
he's severed

doubles in the dirt.
How about

go fuck yourself?
I want to say

before breaking
his nose and walking out

but don't. I get up
and leave him on the couch

he still thinks we'll share
one day when he's too old

and too broke to live
on his own

and we have no choice
but to let him in.

WRITING ROOM

From the only lit room
in the house I listen
to the sound of you

gathering speed
in the hallway,
stumbling toward me

like you're still
dreaming of bucket swings
slicked with rain, already

one of those people
who gets to where
they need to go

a full hour early—
my cup of tea
newly drinkable

and the epistles
of *White Apples*
and the Taste of Stone

just getting good
when I hear
what can only be

you: hurtling, destined
to trip and cry out
in the morning

of the morning,
needing me to come
hold you and sing

with a pen
in my mouth
and an image

evaporating. Instead
you slow down
by the baby gate

and lower yourself
into my writing room
like a child who knows

what they want:
the hole punch
you've just learned

to take apart
and shake, all
the small paper

circles falling out
as you laugh
and call for your

pregnant mother
to join us
in the light.

WHERE WE LAND

Hurt I've asked him
to stop showing up

two hours early,
he tries not

to look at me
when I open the door

and succeeds.
If the newborn's

down for a nap,
it's the toddler

he goes to.
If the toddler's

asleep, too,
it's our forgotten

dog he serenades,
asking how her week

has been and
Did you miss

me as much
as I missed

you? In therapy
I'm asked

if I felt safe
as a child.

In my living
room, my father's

the patron saint
of fun—better

than I am
at make believe

and building
whole cities

out of the blocks
my sister

handed down.
Sometimes I wonder

if he's been
letting himself in

when I'm at work,
looking out

from my desk
at the leaves

waiting like children
to be picked up

and fixated
on the poem about

the dead man
float and the one

about my mother
as a punchline.

Often I find
myself stuck

on this image
of him opening

his dresser drawer
to show me

everything I'd
inherit when he was

gone—confused
I didn't seem excited

and nudging me
to pick something

I could keep
in my room

to begin
remembering him by.

When it's just
the two of us—

Victoria managing
to get both boys

in a bath
before bed—

we don't know
what to say

or how much space
to give: my father

searching the photos
on the fridge

to see if I've added any
of him back

while I kneel
by another basket

of warm clothes
and fold them

like my mother
folded ours, rehearsing

what she'd do
when she was free.

NOTES

"Mondegreen"—Traditionally, the word "mondegreen" refers to a mishearing of a song lyric that gives it new, if unreliable, meaning.

"Prodromal"—According to the Cleveland Clinic, prodromal labor is a type of false labor contraction that can occur during the third trimester of pregnancy. "Prodromal" comes from the Greek word *prodromos*, meaning "running before." This poem is dedicated to my wife, Victoria Elliott.

"Going Home"—In addition to the spread of COVID-19 in 2020, Oregon experienced its worst wildfire season on record, with the Labor Day wildfires burning 1.2 million acres of land and causing air quality to plummet throughout the state. Our son, Jamie Elliott, was born in the midst of it all, on September 14, 2020. This poem is dedicated to him.

"Big Wave Surfer"—This poem is inspired by the first season of the HBO documentary *100 Foot Wave*, which follows big wave surfing pioneer Garrett McNamara as he attempts to surf a 100-foot wave in Nazaré, Portugal.

"Redmond Tells Me What I Feel"—This poem is dedicated to Redmond Reams.

ACKNOWLEDGMENTS

I want to begin by thanking Nate Marshall, who won the Agnes Lynch Starrett Poetry Prize a decade ago and changed my life with a single phone call.

Before I started sending out this book, I tried to prepare myself for the likelihood that it would take years to see the light of day. Then Nate swooped in and, for the first time in my life as a poet, made me feel like I belonged. Thank you, Nate, for your work, your belief in *The Same Man*, and for opening this door.

It is a dream come true for *The Same Man* to be part of the Pitt Poetry Series, and I'm especially grateful to Alex Wolfe, Lesley Rains, Caleb Gill, Nancy Krygowski, and Jeffrey McDaniel for helping me make the most of this moment. Thanks, too, to the poets who've made this past year such an affirming and beautiful one, especially Edgar Kunz, whose poems, generosity, and support have meant the world to me.

I started writing poetry twenty years ago and will always be grateful for my first teachers, who not only fed my love of poetry but also birthed my love of teaching: Chris Segrave-daly, Tina Chang, Cathy Park Hong, Neil Arditi, Jamie McKendrick, and Joan Larkin.

Getting to spend three years writing and teaching at the University of Virginia was one of the greatest gifts of my life. Jeb Livingood and Barbara Moriarty were the one-two punch of warmth and competence we all needed, and I could not have asked for more devoted teachers in Greg Orr, Lisa Russ Spaar, Rita Dove, Debra Nystrom, and Paul Guest. *The Same Man* wouldn't exist without them—without Greg pushing me to go where I was afraid to go, without Lisa's ecstatic warmth and ongoing belief, without Rita sitting with us at her kitchen table and making us feel like we were up for it, without Debra's careful shepherding of my thesis and without Paul telling me early on, "Bobby, it's not too late for us." I also want to thank Mark Doty, who challenged my poems like never before and kept the fire lit, and Dabney Bankert, Laurie Kutchins, and Greg Wrenn for letting me work with their wonderful students at James Madison University.

To the friend who refused to let me give up and helped me believe *The Same Man* had a shot: Michael Dhyne. You're as close as I'll ever get to a brother and the sweetest friend I'll ever have. To Andy Eaton—ours is a friendship I cherish. Thank you for all the calls, poems, and letters.

Thanks, too, to all the writers I learned from, and grew close to, at UVA, especially Michaela Cowgill, Valencia Robin, Ollie Brickman,

Anna Tomlinson, Rob Shapiro, and Nichole LeFebvre for the abiding camaraderie and support.

Submitting packets of poems is a leap of faith and I want to thank the editors and readers at the journals who first gave these poems a home:

> *BOAAT*, "Man at the Bar"; *Cortland Review*, "Before Anyone Else Knew"; *Diode*, "Harmless"; *Frozen Sea*, "Prodromal" and "What We See Together"; *Hampden-Sydney Poetry Review*, "Together"; *North American Review*, "Lullaby"; *North Dakota Quarterly*, "New Parents" and "Inventory Control"; *Ocean State Review*, "Weekend Getaway" and "Redmond Tells Me What I Feel"; *On the Seawall*, "Initiation"; *ONLY POEMS*, "When I Am Not Thinking of My Father," "Going Home," "Skin to Skin," "Photographs," "The Same Man," and "Where We Land"; *Poet Lore*, "Sounds"; *Poetry Northwest*, "We Hold Each Other in the Kitchen"; *Revel*, "Game Plan" and "Big Wave Surfer"; *RHINO*, "Mondegreen"; and *Shō Poetry Journal*, "The Fall of 1990."

To my parents: through it all, you never once questioned this path. It would have been easy to do, and I'm deeply grateful that you let me chase my dreams on the page and beyond.

To my sister, Emily: Sometimes I say I moved across the country on a whim, but, really, it was to be closer to you. Thank you for paving the way and always giving me an example to follow.

And, finally, to the three who shape my days: Jamie, Peter, and Victoria.

So much is said about how parenting pulls us away from the things we love—art making included—but not enough is said about what it makes possible. You are the great loves of my life, and *The Same Man* is for you.

Jamie, our beloved, our firstborn, you are a miraculously beautiful child and the person who teaches me, day in and day out, what it means to love.

Peter, I finished this book with you in my arms. You turned us into a quartet, and now I'm not sure how we ever got on without you.

And Victoria, my only wish is that we met sooner in life. The past eleven years have been defined by bliss, and you will always be where it all begins.